table of contents

introduction

This journal was created for you—mothers of all kinds, both biological and non-biological—to capture the moments that have shaped your life.

Our legacy and wisdom can only be treasured by future generations if we take the time to share our life stories.

Tell Me Your Life Story, Mum serves as a tool to help you write your thoughts, stories, and reflections, turning this guided journal into a priceless treasure to share with your children, loved ones, and future generations.

The engaging, thought-provoking prompts make it simple to record everything from memories of your childhood and life lessons to your hopes for the future.

Once completed, this book will help your children and future generations gain a fuller understanding of your family's origins.

Most valuably, though, this journal will tell your life story. It's what your family will learn about you and will help you connect with them in a meaningful way. This timeless keepsake is also your chance to inspire the next generation and generations to come with your experiences, accomplishments, and life lessons.

Additional FREE Resources

www.questionsaboutme.com/story

ACCESS THE FREE PRINTABLE LIBRARY FOR:

Editable family tree

Replacement and additional questions (short and detailed)

Lined pages to answer questions and insert into the book

Like our Facebook page
@QuestionsAboutMe

Follow us on Instagram
@QuestionsAboutMe_Official

Questions & Customer Service
hello@questionsaboutme.com

Tell Me Your Life Story, Mum

by Questions About Me™

www.questionsaboutme.com

getting the most out of this journal

Just remember there are no strict rules for using or completing this guided journal.

The format of this book is flexible, and the questions can be tackled in any way. Start from anywhere you like, and fill in your answers in any order. You can skip around and answer questions, or you can start at the beginning and work through them in order.

There is no right or wrong way to respond to each question. You may choose not to answer some questions, and some questions may simply not apply to you. Feel free to use the additional questions available from our website in place of these questions.

Try not to overthink or hold back when answering the questions; instead, write freely and record whatever comes into your mind and heart. Where possible, try to be honest, thoughtful, and detailed in the answers you give to all the questions. There's no need to be formal or worry about structuring your answer perfectly. The best answers are the ones that are unedited and come straight from your heart.

HINT

Be specific wherever you can be. Precise details help make your story come alive. Use both first and last names wherever possible. Also, try for as many exact dates, locations, and addresses, as well as brand names, etc. as possible. Try writing "...the mist-green 1950 Chevy" instead of "...Dad's car," and "...pink peonies" instead of "...flowers." Try "... at Starbucks on Seventh Street, downtown" rather than just "...at Starbucks" to paint a clear picture with your words.

Take your time with answering the questions. As there are a lot of questions, you may want to complete the book over multiple sessions, perhaps dedicating some time each day over a period of weeks or months to complete them.

You may even find it enjoyable to have a family member help set up a video camera or audio recording equipment and have them ask you the questions out loud then record your answers.

If you need additional space to answer a question, you can utilize the extra notes pages at the end of each section. You can also use the notes pages to answer the replacement or additional questions from our website or use them as a space to include some memorable photos.

Go easy on yourself and enjoy the process!

•••

my details
& time capsule

my details

FULL NAME

DATE OF BIRTH

PLACE OF BIRTH	EYE COLOUR
HEIGHT	HAIR COLOUR

DISTINGUISHING MARKS

ATTACH YOUR BABY PHOTO HERE

time capsule

TODAY'S DATE

POPULATION OF YOUR CITY	POPULATION OF YOUR COUNTRY
LEADER OF YOUR COUNTRY	POPULATION OF THE WORLD

THE PRICE OF...

GALLON/BOTTLE OF MILK	MAGAZINE
CUP OF COFFEE	BOOK
LOAF OF BREAD	MORTGAGE INTEREST RATE
GALLON OF GAS/ LITRE OF PETROL	AVERAGE WEEKLY WAGE
POSTAGE STAMP	MONTHLY RENT/ MORTGAGE PAYMENT
NEWSPAPER	AVERAGE HOUSE PRICE

CUT AND ATTACH A NEWSPAPER
MASTHEAD FROM TODAY

•••

early years

Were you named after anyone?

_____

_____

_____

_____

_____

_____

_____

Do you like or dislike your name? Why?

_____

_____

_____

_____

_____

_____

_____

If you could choose a different name, what would it be?

_____

_____

_____

_____

_____

_____

_____

_____

How old were your parents when you were born?

_____

_____

_____

_____

Are there any stories you were told about your birth?

_____

_____

_____

_____

_____

_____

_____

_____

_____

_____

_____

_____

_____

_____

_____

Were you a healthy baby, or were there health concerns?

_____

_____

_____

_____

_____

_____

_____

_____

_____

_____

_____

_____

_____

What are some stories your parents have shared
with you about when you were a baby?

_____

_____

_____

_____

_____

_____

_____

_____

_____

What is your earliest memory?

_____

_____

_____

_____

_____

_____

_____

_____

_____

_____

_____

_____

_____

_____

_____

_____

_____

_____

What keepsakes do you have of your early years? (For example, photos, locks of hair, gifts, etc.)

_____

_____

_____

_____

_____

_____

_____

_____

_____

_____

_____

_____

_____

What do you know about the house you lived in as a baby? How long did you live there?

_____

_____

_____

_____

_____

_____

_____

_____

_____

_____

_____

_____

_____

Describe a character or personality trait you inherited from each (or either) of your parents. Be sure to state which parent for each trait.

_____

_____

_____

_____

_____

_____

_____

_____

_____

_____

_____

_____

_____

_____

_____

_____

_____

_____

_____

_____

_____

_____

_____

_____

_____

_____

_____

_____

_____

notes

notes

_____

_____

_____

_____

_____

_____

_____

_____

_____

_____

_____

_____

_____

_____

_____

_____

_____

_____

_____

_____

_____

_____

_____

_____

_____

_____

_____

_____

_____

_____

...

childhood

Did you have special toys or items that were precious to
you, and what's the story of how they came to you?

_____

_____

_____

_____

_____

_____

_____

What type of games did you enjoy playing with
your friends, siblings, or on your own?

_____

_____

_____

_____

_____

_____

_____

_____

What childhood fears do you remember having? For
example, did you think there were monsters under the
bed, or were you afraid of stepping on cracks?

_____

_____

_____

_____

_____

_____

_____

_____

What are some nostalgic smells, sounds, or tastes
that bring you back to childhood?

_____

_____

_____

_____

_____

_____

_____

_____

_____

Describe places where you spent most of your free time when
you were little. Your room? Your backyard? A friend's house?

_____

_____

_____

_____

_____

_____

_____

_____

_____

_____

Did you have your own room growing up?

_____

_____

_____

_____

_____

_____

_____

What did you like or dislike about the area(s) you lived growing up?

_____

_____

_____

_____

_____

_____

_____

_____

What were mealtimes like growing up? Was there a strict routine?

_____

_____

_____

_____

_____

_____

_____

_____

Describe your childhood kitchen—the smells,
tastes, sounds, textures, and colours.

_____

_____

_____

_____

_____

_____

_____

_____

_____

Were there any foods you disliked as a child,
and do you still dislike them today?

_____

_____

_____

_____

_____

_____

_____

What details do you remember about the ritual of bedtime
or bath time? Are there any specific books or songs you
remember your parents reading or singing to you?

_____

_____

_____

_____

_____

_____

_____

_____

Other than your parents, were there any other adult role models
in your childhood? What made them important to you?

_____

_____

_____

_____

_____

_____

_____

_____

What is an activity you used to do with your parents? State
whether it was something you did with either one parent or both,
and describe a memory of enjoying that activity together.

_____

_____

_____

_____

_____

_____

_____

_____

_____

_____

_____

_____

_____

_____

_____

_____

Did you feel connected to *both* of your parents growing
up or one more than the other? Why or why not?

_____

_____

_____

_____

_____

_____

_____

_____

_____

Did your family have any struggles that had to be overcome? Did they try to shield you from them, or did you play an active role in overcoming them?

_____

_____

_____

_____

_____

_____

_____

_____

_____

_____

_____

Were you given an allowance? If so, can you remember
how much it was? What did you spend it on?

_____

_____

_____

_____

_____

_____

Did you have enough money growing up?

_____

_____

_____

_____

_____

_____

_____

_____

Describe the biggest influences in your life during your school years. In what ways did they influence you (good or bad)?

_____

_____

_____

_____

_____

_____

_____

_____

_____

What did you like or dislike most about grade school?

_____

_____

_____

_____

_____

_____

_____

_____

_____

_____

_____

_____

_____

What subject did you wish was taught in school?

_____

_____

_____

_____

_____

What were your favourite subjects in school?

_____

_____

_____

_____

_____

_____

_____

_____

_____

_____

_____

Did you play any sports or instruments, or participate
in any extracurricular school activities?

_____

_____

_____

_____

_____

_____

_____

_____

Which sports teams were you a fan of as a child?

_____

_____

_____

_____

_____

_____

_____

_____

_____

_____

Describe a standout memory or memories from your high school years.

_____
_____
_____
_____
_____
_____
_____
_____
_____
_____
_____
_____
_____
_____
_____

Describe a proud achievement during your childhood or teenage years.

_____
_____
_____
_____
_____
_____
_____
_____
_____
_____
_____
_____
_____
_____
_____
_____

What did you do for fun after school and on weekends?

_____

_____

_____

_____

_____

_____

_____

_____

_____

_____

_____

Did you have a best friend or a close group of friends? Do you
still keep in contact with any of your school friends today?

_____

_____

_____

_____

_____

_____

_____

_____

_____

_____

_____

_____

_____

_____

_____

_____

_____

Did you have any friends whom your parents disapproved of?
What caused their disapproval?

_____

_____

_____

_____

_____

_____

_____

_____

_____

_____

How were you disciplined when you did something to upset
your parents? What did you do when you got in trouble?

_____

_____

_____

_____

_____

_____

_____

_____

_____

_____

_____

_____

_____

_____

_____

_____

_____

Did you go on family vacations? If so, what memories do you have of them?

What special dates did your family celebrate each
year? How did you celebrate them?

_____

_____

_____

_____

_____

_____

_____

Is there a particular childhood birthday party or other celebration
that stands out in your memory? Why does it stand out?

_____

_____

_____

_____

_____

_____

_____

_____

Do you consider your childhood to have been
a happy one? Why or why not?

_____

_____

_____

_____

_____

_____

_____

_____

_____

What advice would you give to your teenage self today?

notes

_____

_____

_____

_____

_____

_____

_____

_____

_____

_____

_____

_____

_____

_____

_____

_____

_____

_____

_____

_____

_____

_____

_____

_____

_____

_____

_____

_____

•••

interests
& pursuits

Did you always have a clear vision of what you wanted to
do in life? Were your career interests influenced by anyone
or anything in particular or did you drift into things?

_____

_____

_____

_____

_____

_____

_____

_____

_____

_____

_____

_____

_____

_____

_____

_____

Did you attend college, trade school, or join the
military? If so, when and where?

_____

_____

_____

_____

_____

_____

_____

What were the highlights of your post-high school experience?

_____

_____

_____

_____

_____

_____

_____

_____

_____

_____

_____

_____

_____

Do you have any regrets about your post-high school
experience? Would you have done anything differently?

_____

_____

_____

_____

_____

_____

_____

_____

_____

_____

_____

_____

_____

_____

Do you have any general thoughts about education, training, or military service that will be helpful to future generations?

_____

_____

_____

_____

_____

_____

_____

_____

_____

_____

_____

_____

_____

_____

_____

_____

_____

_____

_____

_____

_____

_____

_____

_____

_____

_____

What was the first job you had where you earned a
paycheck? How old were you? Did you like it?

_____

_____

_____

_____

_____

_____

_____

_____

_____

_____

_____

How did you get your first job?

_____

_____

_____

_____

_____

_____

_____

_____

_____

_____

_____

_____

_____

_____

_____

_____

Describe what jobs you have had since high school.

_____

_____

_____

_____

_____

_____

_____

_____

_____

_____

_____

_____

_____

_____

_____

_____

_____

_____

What's the best job you've ever had? Why did you enjoy it?

_____

_____

_____

_____

_____

_____

_____

_____

_____

Where was the first place you lived when you left your
parents' home, and did you live there with others?

_____

_____

_____

_____

_____

_____

_____

_____

_____

_____

How old were you when you started wearing make
up? Who taught you how to apply it?

_____

_____

_____

_____

_____

_____

Were you a dedicated follower of fashion? Which clothes, hair,
and makeup fashion trends are most memorable for you?

_____

_____

_____

_____

_____

What pets have you had in your life? What were their names
and what are your fondest memories of them?

_____

_____

_____

_____

_____

_____

_____

_____

_____

_____

_____

_____

_____

_____

What hobbies have you had, or do you have? When
did you start and how did you get into them?

_____

_____

_____

_____

_____

_____

_____

_____

_____

_____

Describe activities you love doing or that bring you joy.

_____

_____

_____

_____

_____

_____

_____

_____

_____

_____

_____

_____

_____

_____

_____

_____

_____

_____

_____

_____

_____

_____

_____

_____

_____

_____

_____

_____

_____

_____

notes

...

family tree

Great Grandfather

Great Grandmother

Great Grandfather

Great Grandmother

Great Grandfather

Great Grandmother

Great Grandfather

Great Grandmother

Grandfather

Grandmother

Grandfather

Grandmother

OUR
**family
tree**

Father

Mother

Sibling

Sibling

Me

Sibling

Sibling

notes

_____

_____

_____

_____

_____

_____

_____

_____

_____

_____

_____

_____

_____

_____

_____

_____

_____

_____

_____

_____

_____

_____

_____

_____

_____

_____

_____

...

family, friends, & relationships

my parents

FIRST NAME

_____

LAST NAME & MAIDEN NAME

_____

DATE OF BIRTH | BIRTH PLACE

EYE COLOUR | HAIR COLOUR

OCCUPATION

_____

FIRST NAME

_____

LAST NAME & MAIDEN NAME

_____

DATE OF BIRTH | BIRTH PLACE

EYE COLOUR | HAIR COLOUR

OCCUPATION

_____

Describe your relationship with each (or either) of your parents while you were growing up. What was it like? How did your relationship change as you became an adult?

_____

_____

_____

_____

_____

_____

_____

_____

_____

_____

_____

_____

_____

_____

_____

_____

_____

_____

_____

_____

_____

_____

_____

_____

_____

_____

_____

_____

_____

_____

What was at least one important thing you learned to
do or appreciate from each of your parents?

_____

_____

_____

_____

_____

_____

_____

_____

_____

_____

_____

_____

_____

_____

_____

_____

_____

_____

_____

_____

_____

_____

_____

_____

_____

_____

my siblings

FIRST NAME

LAST NAME & MAIDEN NAME

DATE OF BIRTH	BIRTH PLACE
EYE COLOUR	HAIR COLOUR

OCCUPATION

FIRST NAME

LAST NAME & MAIDEN NAME

DATE OF BIRTH	BIRTH PLACE
EYE COLOUR	HAIR COLOUR

OCCUPATION

FIRST NAME

LAST NAME & MAIDEN NAME

DATE OF BIRTH	BIRTH PLACE
EYE COLOUR	HAIR COLOUR

OCCUPATION

FIRST NAME

LAST NAME & MAIDEN NAME

DATE OF BIRTH	BIRTH PLACE
EYE COLOUR	HAIR COLOUR

OCCUPATION

Which traits do you share with your sibling(s), whether physical
or character? In what way(s) do your traits differ?

_____

_____

_____

_____

_____

_____

_____

_____

_____

_____

_____

_____

_____

_____

_____

_____

_____

_____

_____

_____

_____

_____

_____

_____

_____

_____

Did you get along with your sibling(s) as a child?

_____
_____
_____
_____
_____
_____
_____
_____
_____
_____
_____
_____
_____

In what way(s) has your relationship with your
sibling(s) changed over the years?

_____
_____
_____
_____
_____
_____
_____
_____
_____
_____
_____
_____
_____
_____
_____
_____

my grandparents

FIRST NAME

LAST NAME & MAIDEN NAME

DATE OF BIRTH	BIRTH PLACE
EYE COLOUR	HAIR COLOUR

OCCUPATION

FIRST NAME

LAST NAME & MAIDEN NAME

DATE OF BIRTH	BIRTH PLACE
EYE COLOUR	HAIR COLOUR

OCCUPATION

FIRST NAME

LAST NAME & MAIDEN NAME

DATE OF BIRTH	BIRTH PLACE
EYE COLOUR	HAIR COLOUR

OCCUPATION

FIRST NAME

LAST NAME & MAIDEN NAME

DATE OF BIRTH	BIRTH PLACE
EYE COLOUR	HAIR COLOUR

OCCUPATION

What similar or different character traits or personality traits did you see in your grandparents compared to your parents?

_____

_____

_____

_____

_____

_____

_____

_____

_____

_____

_____

_____

_____

_____

_____

_____

_____

_____

_____

_____

_____

_____

_____

_____

_____

_____

_____

_____

How close are you or were you to your grandparents?
What memories or stories of them can you share?

_____

_____

_____

_____

_____

_____

_____

_____

_____

_____

_____

_____

_____

_____

_____

_____

_____

_____

_____

_____

_____

_____

_____

_____

_____

_____

_____

_____

What's an important lesson you were taught by
either or both of your grandparents?

my children

FIRST NAME

LAST NAME & MAIDEN NAME

DATE OF BIRTH	BIRTH PLACE
EYE COLOUR	HAIR COLOUR

OCCUPATION

FIRST NAME

LAST NAME & MAIDEN NAME

DATE OF BIRTH	BIRTH PLACE
EYE COLOUR	HAIR COLOUR

OCCUPATION

FIRST NAME

LAST NAME & MAIDEN NAME

DATE OF BIRTH	BIRTH PLACE
EYE COLOUR	HAIR COLOUR

OCCUPATION

FIRST NAME

LAST NAME & MAIDEN NAME

DATE OF BIRTH	BIRTH PLACE
EYE COLOUR	HAIR COLOUR

OCCUPATION

Which character traits do you love about each child?

_____
_____
_____
_____
_____
_____
_____
_____
_____
_____
_____
_____
_____
_____
_____
_____
_____
_____
_____
_____
_____
_____
_____
_____
_____
_____
_____
_____
_____

What is your dream for your children and grandchildren?

_____

_____

_____

_____

_____

_____

_____

_____

_____

_____

_____

_____

_____

_____

_____

_____

_____

_____

_____

_____

_____

_____

_____

_____

_____

_____

_____

_____

_____

family

Did you have regular family get-togethers when you were growing up? What format did they take and how many people would come?

_____

_____

_____

_____

_____

_____

_____

_____

_____

Have there ever been any serious arguments or fall-outs among your family members? What caused them, and were they ever resolved?

_____

_____

_____

_____

_____

_____

_____

_____

_____

_____

_____

_____

_____

_____

Which people in your life do you consider to be like
family, and what connects them to you?

_____

_____

_____

_____

_____

_____

_____

_____

_____

_____

_____

_____

_____

_____

_____

_____

_____

_____

_____

_____

_____

_____

_____

_____

_____

friends

Who are (or have been) your closest and dearest friends in
life, and what stories do you have of your friendships?

_____
_____
_____
_____
_____
_____
_____
_____
_____
_____
_____
_____
_____
_____
_____
_____
_____
_____
_____
_____
_____
_____
_____
_____
_____
_____

Who is your oldest friend and how many years have you been friends?

_____

_____

_____

_____

_____

_____

_____

_____

_____

_____

_____

Describe a time when a friendship disappointed you
or caused you pain. Was there a resolution?

_____

_____

_____

_____

_____

_____

_____

_____

_____

_____

_____

_____

_____

_____

_____

Who do you (or did you) always go to for advice, and
what is a good example of their great advice?

_____

_____

_____

_____

_____

_____

_____

_____

_____

_____

_____

_____

_____

_____

_____

_____

_____

_____

_____

_____

_____

_____

_____

relationships

How old were you when you went on your first proper
date? Whom was it with and where did you go?

_____

_____

_____

_____

_____

_____

_____

_____

_____

_____

_____

Do you have any personal love stories that you want to share?
For example, your first crush or a breakup story?

_____

_____

_____

_____

_____

_____

_____

_____

_____

_____

_____

_____

How and when did you meet your current partner?

What qualities do you love most about your partner?

_____
_____
_____
_____
_____
_____
_____
_____
_____
_____
_____
_____
_____
_____
_____
_____
_____
_____
_____
_____
_____
_____
_____
_____
_____
_____
_____

Did you have a wedding celebration? Describe the proposal, wedding day, and favourite memories of your wedding.

_____

_____

_____

_____

_____

_____

_____

_____

_____

_____

_____

_____

_____

_____

_____

_____

_____

_____

_____

_____

_____

_____

_____

_____

_____

_____

_____

_____

_____

_____

_____

Based on your experiences, what relationship advice
would you like to pass on to future generations?

_____
_____
_____
_____
_____
_____
_____
_____
_____
_____
_____
_____
_____
_____
_____
_____
_____
_____
_____
_____
_____
_____
_____
_____
_____
_____
_____
_____

notes

notes

_____

_____

_____

_____

_____

_____

_____

_____

_____

_____

_____

_____

_____

_____

_____

_____

_____

_____

_____

_____

_____

_____

_____

_____

_____

_____

_____

•••

motherhood

Describe when you first knew you were going
to be a mum. How did you feel?

_____

_____

_____

_____

_____

_____

_____

_____

_____

_____

_____

Do you have any stories of how family and friends reacted
to the news that you were going to be a mum?

_____

_____

_____

_____

_____

_____

_____

_____

_____

_____

_____

_____

_____

In what ways did becoming a mum change your life?

_____

_____

_____

_____

_____

_____

_____

_____

_____

_____

_____

_____

_____

_____

What aspects of motherhood were challenging for you?

_____

_____

_____

_____

_____

_____

_____

_____

_____

_____

_____

_____

_____

_____

_____

In what ways did your expectations of being a mum
differ from your experience of being a mum?

_____

_____

_____

_____

_____

_____

_____

_____

_____

_____

_____

_____

_____

How did your upbringing influence the way you raised your children?

_____

_____

_____

_____

_____

_____

_____

_____

_____

_____

_____

_____

_____

_____

Which stages of being a mum (for example, toddler, school years, etc.) have you enjoyed most, and which stages have you found most challenging? Why?

_____

_____

_____

_____

_____

_____

_____

_____

_____

_____

_____

_____

_____

Which experiences or memories of being a mum always make you smile?

_____

_____

_____

_____

_____

_____

_____

_____

_____

_____

_____

_____

_____

_____

_____

_____

With hindsight, what advice would you give yourself
today as a new mum and as a parent?

_____

_____

_____

_____

_____

_____

_____

_____

_____

_____

_____

_____

_____

_____

_____

_____

_____

_____

_____

_____

_____

_____

_____

_____

_____

_____

_____

_____

notes

notes

•••

beliefs
& values

What were your parents' spiritual or religious beliefs and affiliations? Did they change over time? What influence have these had in your life? Have you maintained the same beliefs?

_____

_____

_____

_____

_____

_____

_____

_____

_____

_____

_____

_____

How have your spiritual or religious beliefs and affiliations evolved during your life?

_____

_____

_____

_____

_____

_____

_____

_____

_____

_____

_____

_____

What makes you feel most patriotic (or not) about the land of your birth?

_____

_____

_____

_____

_____

_____

What influences have shaped your political beliefs, and
have you always maintained the same beliefs?

_____

_____

_____

_____

_____

_____

_____

_____

_____

_____

_____

Have you ever felt strongly enough about something to take part
in a protest march? If not, what issues would motivate you to?

_____

_____

_____

_____

_____

_____

_____

_____

Are there any ways in which changes in your view of the world have changed the way you live your life? (For example, recycling, boycotting certain products, ditching certain habits etc.)

_____

_____

_____

_____

_____

_____

_____

_____

_____

_____

_____

Do you support any charities? If so, why are these causes important to you?

_____

_____

_____

_____

_____

_____

_____

_____

_____

_____

_____

_____

_____

_____

_____

What do you consider to be your core values in life? What values do you most want to pass on to future generations in your family?

_____

_____

_____

_____

_____

_____

_____

_____

_____

_____

_____

_____

_____

_____

_____

_____

_____

_____

_____

_____

_____

_____

_____

_____

_____

_____

_____

_____

_____

_____

notes

...

reflections

How would you describe yourself?

Is there anything in your family's medical history that
your children or grandchildren should know?

_____

_____

_____

_____

_____

_____

_____

_____

_____

Of all the places you have lived, which one do you look
back on with the fondest memories? Why is this?

_____

_____

_____

_____

_____

_____

_____

_____

_____

_____

_____

_____

_____

_____

_____

_____

Do you have a favourite age or stage in your life?

_____

_____

_____

_____

_____

_____

_____

_____

Who has been the most influential person in your
life? In what ways have they influenced you?

_____

_____

_____

_____

_____

_____

_____

_____

_____

_____

_____

_____

_____

_____

_____

_____

_____

_____

_____

Have you ever given or been the recipient of a random act of kindness?

_____

_____

_____

_____

_____

_____

_____

_____

_____

_____

_____

If you could see into the future, what would you want to find out?

_____

_____

_____

_____

_____

_____

_____

_____

_____

_____

_____

_____

_____

_____

_____

_____

_____

_____

Describe one of the best days you can remember.

_____

_____

_____

_____

_____

_____

_____

_____

_____

_____

_____

_____

_____

_____

_____

_____

_____

_____

_____

_____

_____

_____

_____

_____

Excluding your children, what do you consider to have been your greatest achievement in life so far?

_____

_____

_____

_____

_____

_____

_____

_____

_____

_____

_____

_____

_____

_____

_____

_____

_____

_____

_____

_____

_____

_____

_____

_____

_____

_____

_____

_____

_____

_____

_____

_____

Do you have any regrets in your life? Do you still
hope you will be able to make them right?

_____

_____

_____

_____

_____

_____

_____

_____

_____

_____

_____

_____

Have any events or happenings that you thought were
major issues turned out to be blessings in disguise?

_____

_____

_____

_____

_____

_____

_____

_____

_____

_____

_____

_____

_____

Has anything happened in your lifetime (personal or global)
that you hope future generations never go through?

_____

_____

_____

_____

_____

_____

_____

_____

_____

What's one of the most stressful times you've had to
endure in your life and how did you handle it?

_____

_____

_____

_____

_____

_____

_____

_____

_____

_____

_____

_____

_____

_____

_____

Describe a scary moment in your life. How did you overcome
this and what did you learn from the experience?

_____

_____

_____

_____

_____

_____

_____

_____

_____

_____

_____

Is there anything you've experienced in your life that you think
everyone should experience? If so, what, and for what reasons?

_____

_____

_____

_____

_____

_____

_____

_____

_____

_____

_____

_____

_____

What are some of the most amazing experiences
that have happened to you?

_____

_____

_____

_____

_____

_____

_____

_____

_____

_____

_____

_____

_____

_____

_____

_____

_____

_____

_____

_____

_____

_____

_____

_____

_____

_____

_____

_____

_____

_____

What is one trait you have that you would most like to improve upon?

_____
_____
_____
_____
_____
_____
_____
_____
_____
_____
_____
_____

What secrets do you believe help to create a fulfilling life?

_____
_____
_____
_____
_____
_____
_____
_____
_____
_____
_____
_____
_____
_____
_____
_____

What's the best advice you've received?

What would you want your great-grandchildren and
future generations to know about you?

_____

_____

_____

_____

_____

_____

_____

_____

_____

_____

_____

_____

_____

_____

_____

_____

_____

_____

_____

_____

_____

_____

_____

_____

_____

_____

From your experiences, what life lessons or advice
would you want to share with others?

notes

_____
_____
_____
_____
_____
_____
_____
_____
_____
_____
_____
_____
_____
_____
_____
_____
_____
_____
_____
_____
_____
_____
_____
_____
_____
_____
_____
_____
_____
_____

•••

short questions

my firsts

What was your first word?

How old were you when you had your first kiss?

When was the first time you fell in love?

What was the first movie you saw in a movie theatre?

At what age did you first try alcohol?

How old were you when you first drove a car?

What make and model was your first car? Did you name it?

What was the first record (or tape, CD, or another format) you bought?

Which artist/band was playing at the first concert you went to?

Where did you go on your first vacation without your parents?

Where did you go for your first job interview?

Who was the first non-family member you cooked a meal for?

When and where was your first car ding or fender bender?

Where did you go on your first airplane flight?

What's the first country you visited outside your birth country?

my top five...

Most memorable places you've visited

1. _____

2. _____

3. _____

4. _____

5. _____

Best attributes

1. _____

2. _____

3. _____

4. _____

5. _____

Most listened to singers, bands or musicians?

1. _____

2. _____

3. _____

4. _____

5. _____

Pieces of advice you would give your 16-year-old self

1. _____

2. _____

3. _____

4. _____

5. _____

Famous people (dead or alive) you would most like to meet

1. _____
2. _____
3. _____
4. _____
5. _____

Favourite ice cream flavours

1. _____
2. _____
3. _____
4. _____
5. _____

Things you would do if you had a multi-million-dollar lottery win

1. _____
2. _____
3. _____
4. _____
5. _____

Best presents you remember receiving

1. _____
2. _____
3. _____
4. _____
5. _____

my favourite...

COLOUR	FLOWER
MOVIE SNACK	BOOK
HOT DRINK	SPORT TO PLAY AND/OR WATCH
SEASON OF THE YEAR	BOARD OR CARD GAME
WAY TO SPEND A SUNDAY	BEDTIME STORY AS A CHILD
CANDY OR CHOCOLATE BAR	RESTAURANT AND ITEM ON THE MENU
ACTOR OR ACTRESS	MOVIE
WAY TO UNWIND AFTER A HARD DAY	COCKTAIL OR NON-ALCOHOLIC DRINK
CITY YOU'VE VISITED	ANNUAL CELEBRATION, EXCLUDING YOUR BIRTHDAY
DESSERT OR CAKE	SMELL

quick questions

Do you have a lucky number? If so, what is it?

_____

_____

_____

What type of weather do you love most?

_____

_____

_____

Do you have a valid passport?

_____

_____

_____

What food do you like to have made for you when you're sick?

_____

_____

_____

Are you a morning person or an evening person?

_____

_____

_____

Do you buy lottery tickets? If so, do you always choose the same numbers?

_____

_____

_____

If you could snap your fingers and become an expert
in something, what would you want it to be?

_____

_____

_____

_____

Who or what can always make you laugh?

_____

_____

_____

If you were granted three wishes, what would they be?

_____

_____

_____

What simple pleasures of life do you truly enjoy?

_____

_____

_____

_____

Have you ever won any competition prizes?

_____

_____

_____

What is the most expensive or extravagant thing you have ever bought?

_____

_____

_____

_____

Where did you go on the longest road trip you've ever been on?

_____

_____

_____

_____

What is the farthest you have ever traveled?

_____

_____

_____

_____

Are you superstitious?

_____

_____

_____

What is one of your worst habits?

_____

_____

_____

_____

Do you prefer to be spontaneous or think things through first?

_____

_____

_____

_____

Have you ever broken any bones?

_____

_____

_____

What do you procrastinate over most?

_____

_____

_____

Do you believe in fate?

_____

_____

_____

What in life do you consider to be a waste of money?

_____

_____

_____

_____

_____

_____

_____

What is the most romantic thing anyone has ever done for you?

_____

_____

_____

_____

_____

Do you have a favourite proverb or inspirational
quote that you like to live by?

_____

_____

_____

_____

_____

What makes a birthday special for you?

_____

_____

_____

_____

_____

What famous or important people have you encountered
in real life and how did you meet them?

_____

_____

_____

_____

What is your ideal vacation?

_____

_____

_____

_____

_____

_____

Describe your dream home. Where is it? How
big is it? What features does it have?

_____

_____

_____

_____

_____

_____

_____

_____

_____

List the cities you've lived in throughout your life so far.

_____

_____

_____

_____

_____

_____

_____

_____

_____

_____

_____

_____

List the top ten places on your bucket list you would visit
if resources (money and time) were not a concern.

_____

_____

_____

_____

_____

_____

_____

_____

_____

_____

_____

_____

_____

_____

...

notes to
loved ones

notes to loved ones

THIS IS A
SPACE
FOR YOU TO
WRITE NOTES
TO YOUR
LOVED ONES

notes to loved ones

notes to loved ones

_____
_____
_____
_____
_____
_____
_____
_____
_____
_____
_____
_____
_____
_____
_____
_____
_____
_____
_____
_____
_____
_____
_____
_____
_____
_____
_____
_____
_____

notes to loved ones

notes to loved ones

_____

_____

_____

_____

_____

_____

_____

_____

_____

_____

_____

_____

_____

_____

_____

_____

_____

_____

_____

_____

_____

_____

_____

_____

_____

_____

_____

_____

_____

About Us

We're an odd bunch of fun, quirky, and creative authors who love writing thought-provoking questions.

We've all experienced awkward silence situations and resorted to superficial chitchat and small talk to pass time.

The authors here at Questions About Me are on a mission to end dull conversations. We created the *Questions About Me* series to invigorate conversations and help you get to know people better—including yourself.

The *Tell Me Your Life Story* series helps capture your experiences, life stories, and reflections into a timeless keepsake to share with your children, loved ones, and future generations.

Put down your phone, switch off the TV, and use our books to unlock endless conversational possibilities, develop deeper relationships, and create precious memories.

www.questionsaboutme.com

Also by Questions About Me

TELL ME YOUR LIFE STORY SERIES

Tell Me Your Life Story, Mum

Tell Me Your Life Story, Dad

Tell Me Your Life Story, Grandma

Tell Me Your Life Story, Grandad

QUESTIONS ABOUT ME SERIES

3000 Unique Questions About Me

2000 Unique Questions About Me

1000 Unique Questions About Me

3000 Would You Rather Questions About Me

2000 Would You Rather Questions About Me

1000 Would You Rather Questions About Me

Printed in Great Britain
by Amazon

53297214R00071